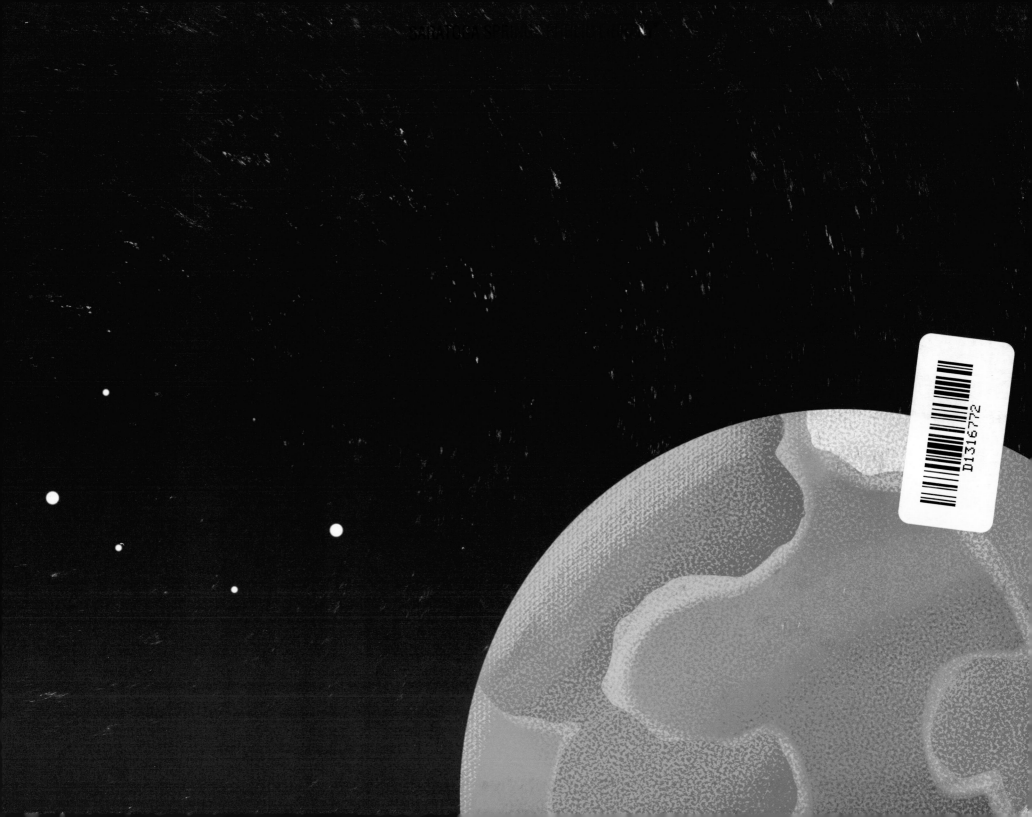

AROUND THE WORLD

One day, when the sky
was gray as the road,

Mama came home

with her bad-mood-down-lips.

I think she needed to sit.

So it wasn't great when
Ollie's spaghetti decided
to fly off his fork,
and WHOA—

SPLAT!

see
you
soon
moon

...a bunch of his lunch
wiggled on top
of Mama's new hat.

And that's why
Mama **grrrrrumped** at Ollie.

And that's why...

Ollie shouted at me,
"Tippi, *I* want to ride the orange scooter!"
And he stuck out his toes so I wouldn't go.

And

that's

why...

I grrrrrouched at Daddy when he rode his bike through the sunflowers, wearing his silly smiley-face shorts, and—

"Beep-beep! Hey-hey! Daddy, puh-leeze get out of my way!"

And that's why...

Daddy got snappy with Sweetie,
our doggie with strawberry spots,
when she put herself under Daddy's feeties.

Sweetie barked at the skunk
that had slunk
under the bushes outside.

And that's why...

The skunk sprayed!

PEE-YEW-EE!

And that's why...

Two sunny songbirds,
caught in a cloud
of skunk juice,
howled out loud,
"ICKKKY OOOH!
We're really not happy
about this goo!"

And off they flew—

...over oceans, and mountains,
   and bridges, and castles on hills.
      And wherever they stopped, they still
         stunk from the skunk, which meant
            some *bad-BAD-stinky-bad* moods
               landed in a lot of places.

In two days, *icky-sticky-picky* grumpies spread

from Mama,   to me,

                        to Ollie,

to Daddy,

and
two songbirds—

to Sweetie,

to one skunk,

...to hundreds of flamingos,

thousands of penguins,

and even to people who live with cows,
all across America, Antarctica, and Mongolia—and WOW!
That's a lot of *ewwey-stewwey-cranky-with-youeey* bad moods!

In seven days, snnipppy, snnarrrly, grrrummbbly, grrrowwly *maminals* (the way Ollie says animals),

and extraterrestrials who only whisper,

and humanoids who are kind of human but sometimes have tails,

Wait a silly second, I said to myself.

Soon, every living thing in the whole universe will be stuck in the yuck of a yuck-ity hufffff! (And that includes trees.)

What can I do? I wondered,
because sometimes, I like to
swing and wonder in my tree,
and all the time, I love
when people find
a way to be kind
and nice to everyone.

Right?

So I sure don't want crummy moods
flying all over the place,
because I'm pretty sure
you can catch a mood
just like a cold when,
HA-CHOO! —
someone sneezes in your face.

HA-CHOO!

So NO thankie
to the Crankies!

And
that's why...

Tonight, when Mama came home and needed to rest her head,

and my yellow-eyed iguana was napping on her bed, I said, "Hey Ma! Get ready, because here comes...

...a HUG!"

And then I gave her a
lovel-you-snuggle-you-huggle-you hug!

And guess what?

No more
bad-mood-down-lips!

They went up like a cup!

And look!
An *I-love-you* smile
woke up Mama's tired eyes!

And guess what?

Mama scooped banana and blueberry ice cream for everyone!

And that's why...

Ollie told Daddy he was as yummy as ice-cream-soup!

And that's why...

Daddy kissed Mama...

...and petted Sweetie
for a long time.

And that's why...

Sweetie left a cookie for the skunk in the bushes.

And that's why...

The skunk listened quietly
to the songbirds sing.

And that's why...

The songbirds sang sunny songs across the skies —

through clouds,

and rains,

and storms of sand,

over deserts,

and smiling giraffes.

and islands,

In two days, easy-breezy-let's-play happy moods blew

from me,

to Mama,

to Ollie,

to Daddy,

to Sweetie,

to one skunk,

and two songbirds—

...to hundreds of monkeys,

thousands of bees,

In seven days,
smiling *maminals* and people
of all colors, shapes, costumes, and hair,

and invisible spirits, far and near,
were sending *happy-clappy-yay* cheer
into the air of e v e r y w h e r e !

Soon, I think, all living things in the whole universe
will be so happy, you will see them
hopping, and twirling, and leaping for stars!

♪ Tra-la-la and ha-ha-ha! ♫

The seas will be glowing; peas will be growing!

And cockatoos
and Sweetie, too,
will be singing
out of the window
and into the wind!

And we'll all be hugging our families and friends.

(And that includes frogs.)

And just to make sure that
my *dancing-prancing* spirit
reaches places like Zanzibar,
Bali, Oz, and the moon,

I plan on hugging Ollie, too!

Hey, today when I was standing
upside-down outside the house,
I saw a bunny hug a mouse,
so I think that hug
may have started with me.

Or maybe
it started
with you?

How I Sent My Hug Around the World
by Donna Ellen Conrad; illustrated by Monez Gusmang

Summary:
A young girl discovers that a single hug can
spread happiness to every living thing in the universe,
reversing the contagion of crankiness that began in her family.

Published by:
Hummingbird Book Press
Hummingbird eBooks
contact: info@hummingbirdbookpress.com

First Edition Hard Copy 2015
Printed in PRC

Library of Congress Control Number: 2015908369

For the reproduction of his painting,
we acknowledge the artist, David Alan Conrad (1949-2012).

Publisher's Cataloging-in-Publication Data

Conrad, Donna Ellen.
   How I sent my hug around the world / Donna Ellen
Conrad ; [illustrated by]   Monez Gusmang.
     pages cm
   ISBN: 978-0-9852457-1-9 (hardcover)
   ISBN: 978-0-9852457-3-3 (pbk.)
   ISBN: 978-0-9852457-2-6 (e-book)
   1. Hugging—Fiction. 2. Conduct of life—Fiction. 3.
Cheerfulness—Fiction. 4. Picture books for children.   I.
Gusmang, Monez, illustrator. II. Title.
PZ7.1.C66   Ho   2015
[Fic]—dc23
                                        2015908369

For my family:
Zakary, Gaudia, and Russell,
and for all the spirits in the wings.
And for Bali, treasure of my soul.
— Donna Ellen Conrad

For my family :
Gek Ami and Gus Bama
— Monez Gusmang

Acknowledgements:
Big hugs for those who added their time and love:
Russell Carpenter, Zakary Selbert, Gaudia Correia,
Ton Huijbers, Viebeke Lengkong,
Richard Souza, Gek Ami.

Above all, for bringing his Balinese spirit into my life
and making this a work of love, fun, and beauty,
hugs aplenty for Monez Gusmang.

DONNA ELLEN CONRAD

MONEZ GUSMANG